How He Lied to Her Husband

George Bernard Shaw

Contents

HOW HE LIED TO HER HUSBAND

BY

George Bernard Shaw

PREFACE

Like many other works of mine, this playlet is a piece d'occasion. In 1905 it happened that Mr Arnold Daly, who was then playing the part of Napoleon in The Man of Destiny in New York, found that whilst the play was too long to take a secondary place in the evening's performance, it was too short to suffice by itself. I therefore took advantage of four days continuous rain during a holiday in the north of Scotland to write How He Lied To Her Husband for Mr Daly. In his hands, it served its turn very effectively.

I print it here as a sample of what can be done with even the most hackneyed stage framework by filling it in with an observed touch of actual humanity instead of with doctrinaire romanticism. Nothing in the theatre is staler than the situation of husband, wife and lover, or the fun of knockabout farce. I have taken both, and got an original play out of them, as anybody else can if only he will look about him for his material instead of plagiarizing Othello and the thousand plays that have proceeded on Othello's romantic assumptions and false point of honor.

A further experiment made by Mr Arnold Daly with this play is worth recording. In 1905 Mr Daly produced Mrs Warren's Profession in New York. The press of that city instantly raised a cry that such persons as Mrs Warren are "ordure," and should not be mentioned in the presence of decent people. This hideous repudiation of humanity and social conscience so took possession of the New York journalists that the few among them who kept their feet morally and intellectually could do nothing to check the epidemic of foul language, gross suggestion, and raving obscenity of word and thought that broke out. The writers abandoned all self-restraint under the impression that they were upholding virtue instead of outraging it. They infected each other with their hysteria until they were for all practical purposes indecently mad. They finally forced the police to arrest Mr Daly and his company, and led the magistrate to express his loathing of the duty thus forced upon him of reading an unmentionable and abominable play. Of course the convulsion soon exhausted itself. The magistrate, naturally somewhat impatient when he found that what he had to read was a strenuously ethical play forming part of a book which had been in circulation unchallenged for eight years, and had been received without protest by the whole London and New York press, gave the journalists a piece of his mind as to their moral taste in plays. By consent, he passed the case on to a higher court, which declared that the play was not immoral; acquitted Mr Daly; and made an end of the attempt to use the law to declare living women to be "ordure," and thus enforce silence as to the far-reaching fact that you cannot cheapen women in the market for industrial purposes without cheapening them for other purposes as well. I hope Mrs Warren's Profession will be played everywhere, in season and out of season, until Mrs Warren has bitten that fact into the public conscience, and shamed the newspapers which support a tariff to keep up the price of every American commodity except American manhood and womanhood.

Unfortunately, Mr Daly had already suffered the usual fate of those who direct public attention to the profits of the sweater or the pleasures of the voluptuary. He was morally lynched side by side with me. Months elapsed before the decision of the courts vindicated him; and even then, since his vindication implied the condemnation of the press, which was by that time sober again, and ashamed of its orgy, his triumph received a rather sulky and grudging publicity. In the meantime he had hardly been able to approach an American city, including even those cities which had heaped applause on him as the defender of hearth and home when he produced Candida, without having to face articles discussing whether

mothers could allow their daughters to attend such plays as You Never
Can Tell, written by the infamous author of Mrs Warren's Profession, and
acted by the monster who produced it. What made this harder to bear was
that though no fact is better established in theatrical business than
the financial disastrousness of moral discredit, the journalists who had
done all the mischief kept paying vice the homage of assuming that it
is enormously popular and lucrative, and that I and Mr Daly, being
exploiters of vice, must therefore be making colossal fortunes out of
the abuse heaped on us, and had in fact provoked it and welcomed it with
that express object. Ignorance of real life could hardly go further.
One consequence was that Mr Daly could not have kept his financial
engagements or maintained his hold on the public had he not accepted
engagements to appear for a season in the vaudeville theatres [the
American equivalent of our music halls], where he played How He Lied
to Her Husband comparatively unhampered by the press censorship of
the theatre, or by that sophistication of the audience through press
suggestion from which I suffer more, perhaps, than any other author.
Vaudeville authors are fortunately unknown: the audiences see what the
play contains and what the actor can do, not what the papers have told
them to expect. Success under such circumstances had a value both for Mr
Daly and myself which did something to console us for the very unsavory
mobbing which the New York press organized for us, and which was not the
less disgusting because we suffered in a good cause and in the very best
company.
Mr Daly, having weathered the storm, can perhaps shake his soul free
of it as he heads for fresh successes with younger authors. But I have
certain sensitive places in my soul: I do not like that word "ordure."
Apply it to my work, and I can afford to smile, since the world, on the
whole, will smile with me. But to apply it to the woman in the street,
whose spirit is of one substance with our own and her body no less holy:
to look your women folk in the face afterwards and not go out and hang
yourself: that is not on the list of pardonable sins.

POSTSCRIPT. Since the above was written news has arrived from America that a leading New York newspaper, which was among the most abusively clamorous for the suppression of Mrs Warren's Profession, has just been fined heavily for deriving part of its revenue from advertisements of Mrs Warren's houses.

Many people have been puzzled by the fact that whilst stage entertainments which are frankly meant to act on the spectators as aphrodisiacs, are everywhere tolerated, plays which have an almost horrifyingly contrary effect are fiercely attacked by persons and papers notoriously indifferent to public morals on all other occasions. The explanation is very simple. The profits of Mrs Warren's profession are shared not only by Mrs Warren and Sir George Crofts, but by the landlords of their houses, the newspapers which advertize them, the restaurants which cater for them, and, in short, all the trades to which they are good customers, not to mention the public officials and representatives whom they silence by complicity, corruption, or blackmail. Add to these the employers who profit by cheap female labor, and the shareholders whose dividends depend on it [you find such people everywhere, even on the judicial bench and in the highest places in Church and State], and you get a large and powerful class with a strong pecuniary incentive to protect Mrs Warren's profession, and a correspondingly strong incentive to conceal, from their own consciences no less than from the world, the real sources of their gain. These are the people who declare that it is feminine vice and not poverty that drives women to the streets, as if vicious women with independent incomes ever went there. These are the people who, indulgent or indifferent to aphrodisiac plays, raise the moral hue and cry against performances of Mrs Warren's Profession, and drag actresses to the police court to be insulted, bullied, and threatened for fulfilling their engagements. For please observe that the judicial decision in New York State in favor of the play does not end the matter. In Kansas City, for instance, the municipality, finding itself restrained by the courts from preventing the performance, fell back on a local bye-law against indecency to evade the Constitution of the United States. They summoned the actress who impersonated Mrs Warren to the police court, and offered her and her colleagues the alternative of leaving the city or being prosecuted under this bye-law.

Now nothing is more possible than that the city councillors who suddenly displayed such concern for the morals of the theatre were either Mrs Warren's landlords, or employers of women at starvation wages, or restaurant keepers, or newspaper proprietors, or in some other more or less direct way sharers of the profits of her trade. No doubt it is equally possible that they were simply stupid men who thought that indecency consists, not in evil, but in mentioning it. I have, however, been myself a member of a municipal council, and have not found municipal councillors quite so simple and inexperienced as this. At all events I do not propose to give the Kansas councillors the benefit of the doubt. I therefore advise the public at large, which will finally decide the matter, to keep a vigilant eye on gentlemen who will stand anything at the theatre except a performance of Mrs Warren's Profession, and who assert in the same breath that [a] the play is too loathsome to be bearable by civilized people, and [b] that unless its performance is prohibited the whole town will throng to see it. They may be merely excited and foolish; but I am bound to warn the public that it is equally likely that they may be collected and knavish.

At all events, to prohibit the play is to protect the evil which the play exposes; and in view of that fact, I see no reason for assuming that the prohibitionists are disinterested moralists, and that the author, the managers, and the performers, who depend for their livelihood on their personal reputations and not on rents, advertisements, or dividends, are grossly inferior to them in moral sense and public responsibility.

It is true that in Mrs Warren's Profession, Society, and not any individual, is the villain of the piece; but it does not follow that the people who take offence at it are all champions of society. Their credentials cannot be too carefully examined.

HOW HE LIED TO HER HUSBAND

It is eight o'clock in the evening. The curtains are drawn and the lamps lighted in the drawing room of Her flat in Cromwell Road. Her lover, a beautiful youth of eighteen, in evening dress and cape, with a bunch of flowers and an opera hat in his hands, comes in alone. The door is near the corner; and as he appears in the doorway, he has the fireplace on the nearest wall to his right, and the grand piano along the opposite wall to his left. Near the fireplace a small ornamental table has on it a hand mirror, a fan, a pair of long white gloves, and a little white woollen cloud to wrap a woman's head in. On the other side of the room, near the piano, is a broad, square, softly up-holstered stool. The room is furnished in the most approved South Kensington fashion: that is, it is as like a show room as possible, and is intended to demonstrate the racial position and spending powers of its owners, and not in the least to make them comfortable.

He is, be it repeated, a very beautiful youth, moving as in a dream, walking as on air. He puts his flowers down carefully on the table beside the fan; takes off his cape, and, as there is no room on the table for it, takes it to the piano; puts his hat on the cape; crosses to the hearth; looks at his watch; puts it up again; notices the things on the table; lights up as if he saw heaven opening before him; goes to the table and takes the cloud in both hands, nestling his nose into its softness and kissing it; kisses the gloves one after another; kisses the fan: gasps a long shuddering sigh of ecstasy; sits down on the stool and

presses his hands to his eyes to shut out reality and dream a little;
takes his hands down and shakes his head with a little smile of rebuke
for his folly; catches sight of a speck of dust on his shoes and hastily
and carefully brushes it off with his handkerchief; rises and takes
the hand mirror from the table to make sure of his tie with the gravest
anxiety; and is looking at his watch again when She comes in, much
flustered. As she is dressed for the theatre; has spoilt, petted ways;
and wears many diamonds, she has an air of being a young and beautiful
woman; but as a matter of hard fact, she is, dress and pretensions
apart, a very ordinary South Kensington female of about 37, hopelessly
inferior in physical and spiritual distinction to the beautiful youth,
who hastily puts down the mirror as she enters.

HE [kissing her hand] At last!

SHE. Henry: something dreadful has happened.

HE. What's the matter?

SHE. I have lost your poems.

HE. They were unworthy of you. I will write you some more.

SHE. No, thank you. Never any more poems for me. Oh, how could I have
been so mad! so rash! so imprudent!

HE. Thank Heaven for your madness, your rashness, your imprudence!

SHE [impatiently] Oh, be sensible, Henry. Can't you see what a terrible
thing this is for me? Suppose anybody finds these poems! what will they
think?

HE. They will think that a man once loved a woman more devotedly than ever man loved woman before. But they will not know what man it was.

SHE. What good is that to me if everybody will know what woman it was?

HE. But how will they know?

SHE. How will they know! Why, my name is all over them: my silly, unhappy name. Oh, if I had only been christened Mary Jane, or Gladys Muriel, or Beatrice, or Francesca, or Guinevere, or something quite common! But Aurora! Aurora! I'm the only Aurora in London; and everybody knows it. I believe I'm the only Aurora in the world. And it's so horribly easy to rhyme to it! Oh, Henry, why didn't you try to restrain your feelings a little in common consideration for me? Why didn't you write with some little reserve?

HE. Write poems to you with reserve! You ask me that!

SHE [with perfunctory tenderness] Yes, dear, of course it was very nice of you; and I know it was my own fault as much as yours. I ought to have noticed that your verses ought never to have been addressed to a married woman.

HE. Ah, how I wish they had been addressed to an unmarried woman! how I wish they had!

SHE. Indeed you have no right to wish anything of the sort. They are quite unfit for anybody but a married woman. That's just the difficulty. What will my sisters-in-law think of them?

HE [painfully jarred] Have you got sisters-in-law?

SHE. Yes, of course I have. Do you suppose I am an angel?

HE [biting his lips] I do. Heaven help me, I do--or I did--or [he almost chokes a sob].

SHE [softening and putting her hand caressingly on his shoulder] Listen to me, dear. It's very nice of you to live with me in a dream, and to love me, and so on; but I can't help my husband having disagreeable relatives, can I?

HE [brightening up] Ah, of course they are your husband's relatives: I forgot that. Forgive me, Aurora. [He takes her hand from his shoulder and kisses it. She sits down on the stool. He remains near the table, with his back to it, smiling fatuously down at her].

SHE. The fact is, Teddy's got nothing but relatives. He has eight sisters and six half-sisters, and ever so many brothers--but I don't mind his brothers. Now if you only knew the least little thing about the world, Henry, you'd know that in a large family, though the sisters quarrel with one another like mad all the time, yet let one of the brothers marry, and they all turn on their unfortunate sister-in-law and devote the rest of their lives with perfect unanimity to persuading him that his wife is unworthy of him. They can do it to her very face without her knowing it, because there are always a lot of stupid low family jokes that nobody understands but themselves. Half the time you can't tell what they're talking about: it just drives you wild. There ought to be a law against a man's sister ever entering his house after he's married. I'm as certain as that I'm sitting here that Georgina stole those poems out of my workbox.

HE. She will not understand them, I think.

SHE. Oh, won't she! She'll understand them only too well. She'll understand more harm than ever was in them: nasty vulgar-minded cat!

HE [going to her] Oh don't, don't think of people in that way. Don't think of her at all. [He takes her hand and sits down on the carpet at her feet]. Aurora: do you remember the evening when I sat here at your feet and read you those poems for the first time?

SHE. I shouldn't have let you: I see that now. When I think of Georgina sitting there at Teddy's feet and reading them to him for the first time, I feel I shall just go distracted.

HE. Yes, you are right. It will be a profanation.

SHE. Oh, I don't care about the profanation; but what will Teddy think? what will he do? [Suddenly throwing his head away from her knee]. You don't seem to think a bit about Teddy. [She jumps up, more and more agitated].

HE [supine on the floor; for she has thrown him off his balance] To me Teddy is nothing, and Georgina less than nothing.

SHE. You'll soon find out how much less than nothing she is. If you think a woman can't do any harm because she's only a scandalmongering dowdy ragbag, you're greatly mistaken. [She flounces about the room. He gets up slowly and dusts his hands. Suddenly she runs to him and throws herself into his arms]. Henry: help me. Find a way out of this for me; and I'll bless you as long as you live. Oh, how wretched I am! [She sobs on his breast].

HE. And oh! how happy I am!

SHE [whisking herself abruptly away] Don't be selfish.

HE [humbly] Yes: I deserve that. I think if I were going to the stake with you, I should still be so happy with you that I could hardly feel your danger more than my own.

SHE [relenting and patting his hand fondly] Oh, you are a dear darling boy, Henry; but [throwing his hand away fretfully] you're no use. I want somebody to tell me what to do.

HE [with quiet conviction] Your heart will tell you at the right time. I have thought deeply over this; and I know what we two must do, sooner or later.

SHE. No, Henry. I will do nothing improper, nothing dishonorable. [She sits down plump on the stool and looks inflexible].

HE. If you did, you would no longer be Aurora. Our course is perfectly simple, perfectly straightforward, perfectly stainless and true. We love one another. I am not ashamed of that: I am ready to go out and proclaim it to all London as simply as I will declare it to your husband when you see--as you soon will see--that this is the only way honorable enough for your feet to tread. Let us go out together to our own house, this evening, without concealment and without shame. Remember! we owe something to your husband. We are his guests here: he is an honorable man: he has been kind to us: he has perhaps loved you as well as his prosaic nature and his sordid commercial environment permitted. We owe it to him in all honor not to let him learn the truth from the lips of a scandalmonger. Let us go to him now quietly, hand in hand; bid him farewell; and walk out of the house without concealment and subterfuge, freely and honestly, in full honor and self-respect.

SHE [staring at him] And where shall we go to?

HE. We shall not depart by a hair's breadth from the ordinary natural current of our lives. We were going to the theatre when the loss of the poems compelled us to take action at once. We shall go to the theatre still; but we shall leave your diamonds here; for we cannot afford diamonds, and do not need them.

SHE [fretfully] I have told you already that I hate diamonds; only Teddy insists on hanging me all over with them. You need not preach simplicity to me.

HE. I never thought of doing so, dearest: I know that these trivialities are nothing to you. What was I saying--oh yes. Instead of coming back here from the theatre, you will come with me to my home--now and henceforth our home--and in due course of time, when you are divorced, we shall go through whatever idle legal ceremony you may desire. I attach no importance to the law: my love was not created in me by the law, nor can it be bound or loosed by it. That is simple enough, and sweet enough, is it not? [He takes the flower from the table]. Here are flowers for you: I have the tickets: we will ask your husband to lend us the carriage to show that there is no malice, no grudge, between us. Come!

SHE [spiritlessly, taking the flowers without looking at them, and temporizing] Teddy isn't in yet.

HE. Well, let us take that calmly. Let us go to the theatre as if nothing had happened, and tell him when we come back. Now or three hours hence: to-day or to-morrow: what does it matter, provided all is done in honor, without shame or fear?

SHE. What did you get tickets for? Lohengrin?

HE. I tried; but Lohengrin was sold out for to-night. [He takes out two Court Theatre tickets].

SHE. Then what did you get?

HE. Can you ask me? What is there besides Lohengrin that we two could endure, except Candida?

SHE [springing up] Candida! No, I won't go to it again, Henry [tossing the flower on the piano]. It is that play that has done all the mischief. I'm very sorry I ever saw it: it ought to be stopped.

HE [amazed] Aurora!

SHE. Yes: I mean it.

HE. That divinest love poem! the poem that gave us courage to speak to one another! that revealed to us what we really felt for one another! That--

SHE. Just so. It put a lot of stuff into my head that I should never have dreamt of for myself. I imagined myself just like Candida.

HE [catching her hands and looking earnestly at her] You were right. You are like Candida.

SHE [snatching her hands away] Oh, stuff! And I thought you were just like Eugene. [Looking critically at him] Now that I come to look at you, you are rather like him, too. [She throws herself discontentedly into the nearest seat, which happens to be the bench at the piano. He goes to her].

HE [very earnestly] Aurora: if Candida had loved Eugene she would have gone out into the night with him without a moment's hesitation.

SHE [with equal earnestness] Henry: do you know what's wanting in that play?

HE. There is nothing wanting in it.

SHE. Yes there is. There's a Georgina wanting in it. If Georgina had been there to make trouble, that play would have been a true-to-life tragedy. Now I'll tell you something about it that I have never told you before.

HE. What is that?

SHE. I took Teddy to it. I thought it would do him good; and so it would if I could only have kept him awake. Georgina came too; and you should have heard the way she went on about it. She said it was downright immoral, and that she knew the sort of woman that encourages boys to sit on the hearthrug and make love to her. She was just preparing Teddy's mind to poison it about me.

HE. Let us be just to Georgina, dearest

SHE. Let her deserve it first. Just to Georgina, indeed!

HE. She really sees the world in that way. That is her punishment.

SHE. How can it be her punishment when she likes it? It'll be my punishment when she brings that budget of poems to Teddy. I wish you'd have some sense, and sympathize with my position a little.

HE. [going away from the piano and beginning to walk about rather testily] My dear: I really don't care about Georgina or about Teddy. All these squabbles belong to a plane on which I am, as you say, no use. I have counted the cost; and I do not fear the consequences. After all, what is there to fear? Where is the difficulty? What can Georgina do? What can your husband do? What can anybody do?

SHE. Do you mean to say that you propose that we should walk right bang up to Teddy and tell him we're going away together?

HE. Yes. What can be simpler?

SHE. And do you think for a moment he'd stand it, like that half-baked clergyman in the play? He'd just kill you.

HE [coming to a sudden stop and speaking with considerable confidence] You don't understand these things, my darling, how could you? In one respect I am unlike the poet in the play. I have followed the Greek ideal and not neglected the culture of my body. Your husband would make a tolerable second-rate heavy weight if he were in training and ten years younger. As it is, he could, if strung up to a great effort by a burst of passion, give a good account of himself for perhaps fifteen seconds. But I am active enough to keep out of his reach for fifteen seconds; and after that I should be simply all over him.

SHE [rising and coming to him in consternation] What do you mean by all over him?

HE [gently] Don't ask me, dearest. At all events, I swear to you that you need not be anxious about me.

SHE. And what about Teddy? Do you mean to tell me that you are going to beat Teddy before my face like a brutal prizefighter?

HE. All this alarm is needless, dearest. Believe me, nothing will happen. Your husband knows that I am capable of defending myself. Under such circumstances nothing ever does happen. And of course I shall do nothing. The man who once loved you is sacred to me.

SHE [suspiciously] Doesn't he love me still? Has he told you anything?

HE. No, no. [He takes her tenderly in his arms]. Dearest, dearest: how agitated you are! how unlike yourself! All these worries belong to the lower plane. Come up with me to the higher one. The heights, the solitudes, the soul world!

SHE [avoiding his gaze] No: stop: it's no use, Mr Apjohn.

HE [recoiling] Mr Apjohn!!!

SHE. Excuse me: I meant Henry, of course.

HE. How could you even think of me as Mr Apjohn? I never think of you as Mrs Bompas: it is always Cand-- I mean Aurora, Aurora, Auro--

SHE. Yes, yes: that's all very well, Mr Apjohn [He is about to interrupt again: but she won't have it] no: it's no use: I've suddenly begun to think of you as Mr Apjohn; and it's ridiculous to go on calling you Henry. I thought you were only a boy, a child, a dreamer. I thought you would be too much afraid to do anything. And now you want to beat Teddy and to break up my home and disgrace me and make a horrible scandal in the papers. It's cruel, unmanly, cowardly.

HE [with grave wonder] Are you afraid?

SHE. Oh, of course I'm afraid. So would you be if you had any common sense. [She goes to the hearth, turning her back to him, and puts one tapping foot on the fender].

HE [watching her with great gravity] Perfect love casteth out fear. That is why I am not afraid. Mrs Bompas: you do not love me.

SHE [turning to him with a gasp of relief] Oh, thank you, thank you! You really can be very nice, Henry.

HE. Why do you thank me?

SHE [coming prettily to him from the fireplace] For calling me Mrs Bompas again. I feel now that you are going to be reasonable and behave like a gentleman. [He drops on the stool; covers his face with his hand; and groans]. What's the matter?

HE. Once or twice in my life I have dreamed that I was exquisitely happy and blessed. But oh! the misgiving at the first stir of consciousness! the stab of reality! the prison walls of the bedroom! the bitter, bitter disappointment of waking! And this time! oh, this time I thought I was awake.

SHE. Listen to me, Henry: we really haven't time for all that sort of flapdoodle now. [He starts to his feet as if she had pulled a trigger and straightened him by the release of a powerful spring, and goes past her with set teeth to the little table]. Oh, take care: you nearly hit me in the chin with the top of your head.

HE [with fierce politeness] I beg your pardon. What is it you want me to do? I am at your service. I am ready to behave like a gentleman if you will be kind enough to explain exactly how.

SHE [a little frightened] Thank you, Henry: I was sure you would. You're not angry with me, are you?

HE. Go on. Go on quickly. Give me something to think about, or I will--I will--[he suddenly snatches up her fan and it about to break it in his clenched fists].

SHE [running forward and catching at the fan, with loud lamentation] Don't break my fan--no, don't. [He slowly relaxes his grip of it as she draws it anxiously out of his hands]. No, really, that's a stupid trick.

I don't like that. You've no right to do that. [She opens the fan, and finds that the sticks are disconnected]. Oh, how could you be so inconsiderate?

HE. I beg your pardon. I will buy you a new one.

SHE [querulously] You will never be able to match it. And it was a particular favorite of mine.

HE [shortly] Then you will have to do without it: that's all.

SHE. That's not a very nice thing to say after breaking my pet fan, I think.

HE. If you knew how near I was to breaking Teddy's pet wife and presenting him with the pieces, you would be thankful that you are alive instead of--of--of howling about five shillings worth of ivory. Damn your fan!

SHE. Oh! Don't you dare swear in my presence. One would think you were my husband.

HE [again collapsing on the stool] This is some horrible dream. What has become of you? You are not my Aurora.

SHE. Oh, well, if you come to that, what has become of you? Do you think I would ever have encouraged you if I had known you were such a little devil?

HE. Don't drag me down--don't--don't. Help me to find the way back to the heights.

SHE [kneeling beside him and pleading] If you would only be reasonable,

Henry. If you would only remember that I am on the brink of ruin, and not go on calmly saying it's all quite simple.

HE. It seems so to me.

SHE [jumping up distractedly] If you say that again I shall do something I'll be sorry for. Here we are, standing on the edge of a frightful precipice. No doubt it's quite simple to go over and have done with it. But can't you suggest anything more agreeable?

HE. I can suggest nothing now. A chill black darkness has fallen: I can see nothing but the ruins of our dream. [He rises with a deep sigh].

SHE. Can't you? Well, I can. I can see Georgina rubbing those poems into Teddy. [Facing him determinedly] And I tell you, Henry Apjohn, that you got me into this mess; and you must get me out of it again.

HE [polite and hopeless] All I can say is that I am entirely at your service. What do you wish me to do?

SHE. Do you know anybody else named Aurora?

HE. No.

SHE. There's no use in saying No in that frozen pigheaded way. You must know some Aurora or other somewhere.

HE. You said you were the only Aurora in the world. And [lifting his clasped fists with a sudden return of his emotion] oh God! you were the only Aurora in the world to me. [He turns away from her, hiding his face].

SHE [petting him] Yes, yes, dear: of course. It's very nice of you; and

I appreciate it: indeed I do; but it's not reasonable just at present.
Now just listen to me. I suppose you know all those poems by heart.

HE. Yes, by heart. [Raising his head and looking at her, with a sudden
suspicion] Don't you?

SHE. Well, I never can remember verses; and besides, I've been so busy
that I've not had time to read them all; though I intend to the very
first moment I can get: I promise you that most faithfully, Henry. But
now try and remember very particularly. Does the name of Bompas occur in
any of the poems?

HE [indignantly] No.

SHE. You're quite sure?

HE. Of course I am quite sure. How could I use such a name in a poem?

SHE. Well, I don't see why not. It rhymes to rumpus, which seems
appropriate enough at present, goodness knows! However, you're a poet,
and you ought to know.

HE. What does it matter--now?

SHE. It matters a lot, I can tell you. If there's nothing about Bompas
in the poems, we can say that they were written to some other Aurora,
and that you showed them to me because my name was Aurora too. So you've
got to invent another Aurora for the occasion.

HE [very coldly] Oh, if you wish me to tell a lie--

SHE. Surely, as a man of honor--as a gentleman, you wouldn't tell the
truth, would you?

HE. Very well. You have broken my spirit and desecrated my dreams. I will lie and protest and stand on my honor: oh, I will play the gentleman, never fear.

SHE. Yes, put it all on me, of course. Don't be mean, Henry.

HE [rousing himself with an effort] You are quite right, Mrs Bompas: I beg your pardon. You must excuse my temper. I have got growing pains, I think.

SHE. Growing pains!

HE. The process of growing from romantic boyhood into cynical maturity usually takes fifteen years. When it is compressed into fifteen minutes, the pace is too fast; and growing pains are the result.

SHE. Oh, is this a time for cleverness? It's settled, isn't it, that you're going to be nice and good, and that you'll brazen it out to Teddy that you have some other Aurora?

HE. Yes: I'm capable of anything now. I should not have told him the truth by halves; and now I will not lie by halves. I'll wallow in the honor of a gentleman.

SHE. Dearest boy, I knew you would. I--Sh! [she rushes to the door, and holds it ajar, listening breathlessly].

HE. What is it?

SHE [white with apprehension] It's Teddy: I hear him tapping the new barometer. He can't have anything serious on his mind or he wouldn't do that. Perhaps Georgina hasn't said anything. [She steals back to the hearth]. Try and look as if there was nothing the matter. Give me my gloves, quick. [He hands them to her. She pulls on one hastily and begins buttoning it with ostentatious unconcern]. Go further away from me, quick. [He walks doggedly away from her until the piano prevents his going farther]. If I button my glove, and you were to hum a tune, don't you think that--

HE. The tableau would be complete in its guiltiness. For Heaven's sake, Mrs Bompas, let that glove alone: you look like a pickpocket.

Her husband comes in: a robust, thicknecked, well groomed city man, with a strong chin but a blithering eye and credulous mouth. He has a momentous air, but shows no sign of displeasure: rather the contrary.

HER HUSBAND. Hallo! I thought you two were at the theatre.

SHE. I felt anxious about you, Teddy. Why didn't you come home to dinner?

HER HUSBAND. I got a message from Georgina. She wanted me to go to her.

SHE. Poor dear Georgina! I'm sorry I haven't been able to call on her this last week. I hope there's nothing the matter with her.

HER HUSBAND. Nothing, except anxiety for my welfare and yours. [She steals a terrified look at Henry]. By, the way, Apjohn, I should like a word with you this evening, if Aurora can spare you for a moment.

HE [formally] I am at your service.

HER HUSBAND. No hurry. After the theatre will do.

HE. We have decided not to go.

HER HUSBAND. Indeed! Well, then, shall we adjourn to my snuggery?

SHE. You needn't move. I shall go and lock up my diamonds since I'm not going to the theatre. Give me my things.

HER HUSBAND [as he hands her the cloud and the mirror] Well, we shall have more room here.

HE [looking about him and shaking his shoulders loose] I think I should prefer plenty of room.

HER HUSBAND. So, if it's not disturbing you, Rory--?

SHE. Not at all. [She goes out].

When the two men are alone together, Bompas deliberately takes the poems from his breast pocket; looks at them reflectively; then looks at Henry, mutely inviting his attention. Henry refuses to understand, doing his best to look unconcerned.

HER HUSBAND. Do these manuscripts seem at all familiar to you, may I ask?

HE. Manuscripts?

HER HUSBAND. Yes. Would you like to look at them a little closer? [He proffers them under Henry's nose].

HE [as with a sudden illumination of glad surprise] Why, these are my poems.

HER HUSBAND. So I gather.

HE. What a shame! Mrs Bompas has shown them to you! You must think me an
utter ass. I wrote them years ago after reading Swinburne's Songs Before
Sunrise. Nothing would do me then but I must reel off a set of Songs
to the Sunrise. Aurora, you know: the rosy fingered Aurora. They're all
about Aurora. When Mrs Bompas told me her name was Aurora, I couldn't
resist the temptation to lend them to her to read. But I didn't bargain
for your unsympathetic eyes.

HER HUSBAND [grinning] Apjohn: that's really very ready of you. You are
cut out for literature; and the day will come when Rory and I will be
proud to have you about the house. I have heard far thinner stories from
much older men.

HE [with an air of great surprise] Do you mean to imply that you don't
believe me?

HER HUSBAND. Do you expect me to believe you?

HE. Why not? I don't understand.

HER HUSBAND. Come! Don't underrate your own cleverness, Apjohn. I think
you understand pretty well.

HE. I assure you I am quite at a loss. Can you not be a little more
explicit?

HER HUSBAND. Don't overdo it, old chap. However, I will just be so far
explicit as to say that if you think these poems read as if they were
addressed, not to a live woman, but to a shivering cold time of day at
which you were never out of bed in your life, you hardly do justice to
your own literary powers--which I admire and appreciate, mind you, as

much as any man. Come! own up. You wrote those poems to my wife. [An internal struggle prevents Henry from answering]. Of course you did. [He throws the poems on the table; and goes to the hearthrug, where he plants himself solidly, chuckling a little and waiting for the next move].

HE [formally and carefully] Mr Bompas: I pledge you my word you are mistaken. I need not tell you that Mrs Bompas is a lady of stainless honor, who has never cast an unworthy thought on me. The fact that she has shown you my poems--

HER HUSBAND. That's not a fact. I came by them without her knowledge. She didn't show them to me.

HE. Does not that prove their perfect innocence? She would have shown them to you at once if she had taken your quite unfounded view of them.

HER HUSBAND [shaken] Apjohn: play fair. Don't abuse your intellectual gifts. Do you really mean that I am making a fool of myself?

HE [earnestly] Believe me, you are. I assure you, on my honor as a gentleman, that I have never had the slightest feeling for Mrs Bompas beyond the ordinary esteem and regard of a pleasant acquaintance.

HER HUSBAND [shortly, showing ill humor for the first time] Oh, indeed. [He leaves his hearth and begins to approach Henry slowly, looking him up and down with growing resentment].

HE [hastening to improve the impression made by his mendacity] I should never have dreamt of writing poems to her. The thing is absurd.

HER HUSBAND [reddening ominously] Why is it absurd?

HE [shrugging his shoulders] Well, it happens that I do not admire Mrs Bompas--in that way.

HER HUSBAND [breaking out in Henry's face] Let me tell you that Mrs Bompas has been admired by better men than you, you soapy headed little puppy, you.

HE [much taken aback] There is no need to insult me like this. I assure you, on my honor as a--

HER HUSBAND [too angry to tolerate a reply, and boring Henry more and more towards the piano] You don't admire Mrs Bompas! You would never dream of writing poems to Mrs Bompas! My wife's not good enough for you, isn't she. [Fiercely] Who are you, pray, that you should be so jolly superior?

HE. Mr Bompas: I can make allowances for your jealousy--

HER HUSBAND. Jealousy! do you suppose I'm jealous of YOU? No, nor of ten like you. But if you think I'll stand here and let you insult my wife in her own house, you're mistaken.

HE [very uncomfortable with his back against the piano and Teddy standing over him threateningly] How can I convince you? Be reasonable. I tell you my relations with Mrs Bompas are relations of perfect coldness--of indifference--

HER HUSBAND [scornfully] Say it again: say it again. You're proud of it, aren't you? Yah! You're not worth kicking.

Henry suddenly executes the feat known to pugilists as dipping, and changes sides with Teddy, who it now between Henry and the piano.

HE. Look here: I'm not going to stand this.

HER HUSBAND. Oh, you have some blood in your body after all! Good job!

HE. This is ridiculous. I assure you Mrs. Bompas is quite--

HER HUSBAND. What is Mrs Bompas to you, I'd like to know. I'll tell you what Mrs Bompas is. She's the smartest woman in the smartest set in South Kensington, and the handsomest, and the cleverest, and the most fetching to experienced men who know a good thing when they see it, whatever she may be to conceited penny-a-lining puppies who think nothing good enough for them. It's admitted by the best people; and not to know it argues yourself unknown. Three of our first actor-managers have offered her a hundred a week if she'd go on the stage when they start a repertory theatre; and I think they know what they're about as well as you. The only member of the present Cabinet that you might call a handsome man has neglected the business of the country to dance with her, though he don't belong to our set as a regular thing. One of the first professional poets in Bedford Park wrote a sonnet to her, worth all your amateur trash. At Ascot last season the eldest son of a duke excused himself from calling on me on the ground that his feelings for Mrs Bompas were not consistent with his duty to me as host; and it did him honor and me too. But [with gathering fury] she isn't good enough for you, it seems. You regard her with coldness, with indifference; and you have the cool cheek to tell me so to my face. For two pins I'd flatten your nose in to teach you manners. Introducing a fine woman to you is casting pearls before swine [yelling at him] before SWINE! d'ye hear?

HE [with a deplorable lack of polish] You call me a swine again and I'll land you one on the chin that'll make your head sing for a week.

HER HUSBAND [exploding] What--!

He charges at Henry with bull-like fury. Henry places himself on guard in the manner of a well taught boxer, and gets away smartly, but unfortunately forgets the stool which is just behind him. He falls backwards over it, unintentionally pushing it against the shins of Bompas, who falls forward over it. Mrs Bompas, with a scream, rushes into the room between the sprawling champions, and sits down on the floor in order to get her right arm round her husband's neck.

SHE. You shan't, Teddy: you shan't. You will be killed: he is a prizefighter.

HER HUSBAND [vengefully] I'll prizefight him. [He struggles vainly to free himself from her embrace].

SHE. Henry: don't let him fight you. Promise me that you won't.

HE [ruefully] I have got a most frightful bump on the back of my head. [He tries to rise].

SHE [reaching out her left hand to seize his coat tail, and pulling him down again, whilst keeping fast hold of Teddy with the other hand] Not until you have promised: not until you both have promised. [Teddy tries to rise: she pulls him back again]. Teddy: you promise, don't you? Yes, yes. Be good: you promise.

HER HUSBAND. I won't, unless he takes it back.

SHE. He will: he does. You take it back, Henry?--yes.

HE [savagely] Yes. I take it back. [She lets go his coat. He gets up. So does Teddy]. I take it all back, all, without reserve.

SHE [on the carpet] Is nobody going to help me up? [They each take a hand and pull her up]. Now won't you shake hands and be good?

HE [recklessly] I shall do nothing of the sort. I have steeped myself in lies for your sake; and the only reward I get is a lump on the back of my head the size of an apple. Now I will go back to the straight path.

SHE. Henry: for Heaven's sake--

HE. It's no use. Your husband is a fool and a brute--

HER HUSBAND. What's that you say?

HE. I say you are a fool and a brute; and if you'll step outside with me I'll say it again. [Teddy begins to take off his coat for combat]. Those poems were written to your wife, every word of them, and to nobody else. [The scowl clears away from Bompas's countenance. Radiant, he replaces his coat]. I wrote them because I loved her. I thought her the most beautiful woman in the world; and I told her so over and over again. I adored her: do you hear? I told her that you were a sordid commercial chump, utterly unworthy of her; and so you are.

HER HUSBAND [so gratified, he can hardly believe his ears] You don't mean it!

HE. Yes, I do mean it, and a lot more too. I asked Mrs Bompas to walk out of the house with me--to leave you--to get divorced from you and marry me. I begged and implored her to do it this very night. It was her refusal that ended everything between us. [Looking very disparagingly at him] What she can see in you, goodness only knows!

HER HUSBAND [beaming with remorse] My dear chap, why didn't you say so before? I apologize. Come! Don't bear malice: shake hands. Make him shake hands, Rory.

SHE. For my sake, Henry. After all, he's my husband. Forgive him. Take his hand. [Henry, dazed, lets her take his hand and place it in Teddy's].

HER HUSBAND [shaking it heartily] You've got to own that none of your literary heroines can touch my Rory. [He turns to her and claps her with fond pride on the shoulder]. Eh, Rory? They can't resist you: none of em. Never knew a man yet that could hold out three days.

SHE. Don't be foolish, Teddy. I hope you were not really hurt, Henry. [She feels the back of his head. He flinches]. Oh, poor boy, what a bump! I must get some vinegar and brown paper. [She goes to the bell and rings].

HER HUSBAND. Will you do me a great favor, Apjohn. I hardly like to ask; but it would be a real kindness to us both.

HE. What can I do?

HER HUSBAND [taking up the poems] Well, may I get these printed? It shall be done in the best style. The finest paper, sumptuous binding, everything first class. They're beautiful poems. I should like to show them about a bit.

SHE [running back from the bell, delighted with the idea, and coming between them] Oh Henry, if you wouldn't mind!

HE. Oh, I don't mind. I am past minding anything. I have grown too fast this evening.

SHE. How old are you, Henry?

HE. This morning I was eighteen. Now I am--confound it! I'm quoting that beast of a play [he takes the Candida tickets out of his pocket and tears them up viciously].

HER HUSBAND. What shall we call the volume? To Aurora, or something like
that, eh?

HE. I should call it How He Lied to Her Husband.

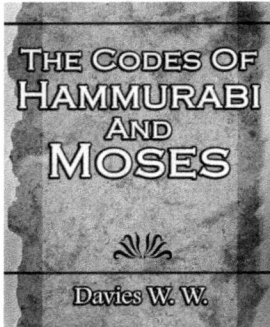

The Codes Of Hammurabi And Moses
W. W. Davies

QTY

The discovery of the Hammurabi Code is one of the greatest achievements of archaeology, and is of paramount interest, not only to the student of the Bible, but also to all those interested in ancient history...

Religion   **ISBN:** *1-59462-338-4*   **Pages:132**
MSRP $12.95

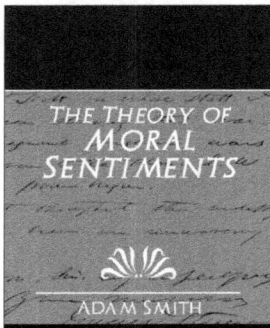

The Theory of Moral Sentiments
Adam Smith

QTY

This work from 1749. contains original theories of conscience amd moral judgment and it is the foundation for systemof morals.

Philosophy   **ISBN:** *1-59462-777-0*   **Pages:536**
MSRP $19.95

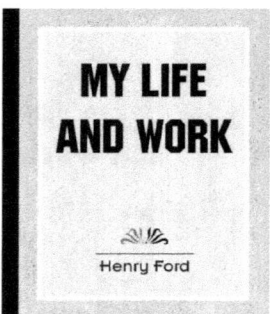

Jessica's First Prayer
Hesba Stretton

QTY

In a screened and secluded corner of one of the many railway-bridges which span the streets of London there could be seen a few years ago, from five o'clock every morning until half past eight, a tidily set-out coffee-stall, consisting of a trestle and board, upon which stood two large tin cans, with a small fire of charcoal burning under each so as to keep the coffee boiling during the early hours of the morning when the work-people were thronging into the city on their way to their daily toil...

Pages:84

Childrens   **ISBN:** *1-59462-373-2*   **MSRP $9.95**

My Life and Work
Henry Ford

QTY

Henry Ford revolutionized the world with his implementation of mass production for the Model T automobile. Gain valuable business insight into his life and work with his own auto-biography... "We have only started on our development of our country we have not as yet, with all our talk of wonderful progress, done more than scratch the surface. The progress has been wonderful enough but..."

Pages:300

Biographies/   **ISBN:** *1-59462-198-5*   **MSRP $21.95**

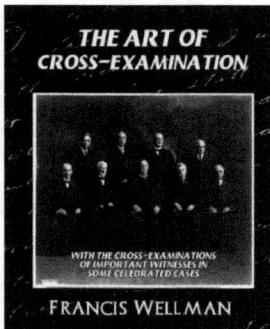

The Art of Cross-Examination
Francis Wellman

QTY

I presume it is the experience of every author, after his first book is published upon an important subject, to be almost overwhelmed with a wealth of ideas and illustrations which could readily have been included in his book, and which to his own mind, at least, seem to make a second edition inevitable. Such certainly was the case with me; and when the first edition had reached its sixth impression in five months, I rejoiced to learn that it seemed to my publishers that the book had met with a sufficiently favorable reception to justify a second and considerably enlarged edition. ..

Pages:412

Reference   ISBN: *1-59462-647-2*   *MSRP $19.95*

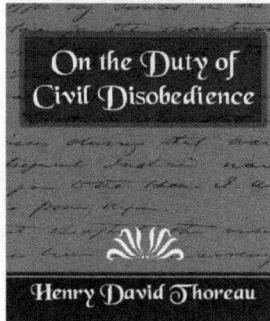

On the Duty of Civil Disobedience
Henry David Thoreau

QTY

Thoreau wrote his famous essay, On the Duty of Civil Disobedience, as a protest against an unjust but popular war and the immoral but popular institution of slave-owning. He did more than write—he declined to pay his taxes, and was hauled off to gaol in consequence. Who can say how much this refusal of his hastened the end of the war and of slavery ?

Law   ISBN: *1-59462-747-9*   **Pages:48**
MSRP $7.45

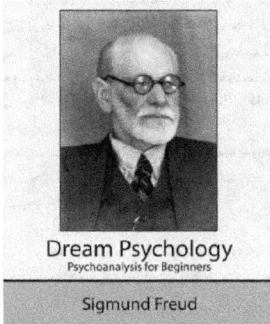

Dream Psychology Psychoanalysis for Beginners
Sigmund Freud

QTY

Sigmund Freud, born Sigismund Schlomo Freud (May 6, 1856 - September 23, 1939), was a Jewish-Austrian neurologist and psychiatrist who co-founded the psychoanalytic school of psychology. Freud is best known for his theories of the unconscious mind, especially involving the mechanism of repression; his redefinition of sexual desire as mobile and directed towards a wide variety of objects; and his therapeutic techniques, especially his understanding of transference in the therapeutic relationship and the presumed value of dreams as sources of insight into unconscious desires.

Pages:196

Psychology   ISBN: *1-59462-905-6*   *MSRP $15.45*

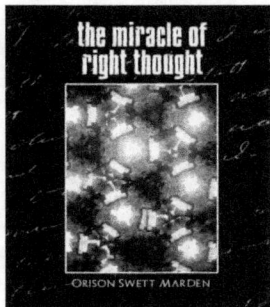

The Miracle of Right Thought
Orison Swett Marden

QTY

Believe with all of your heart that you will do what you were made to do. When the mind has once formed the habit of holding cheerful, happy, prosperous pictures, it will not be easy to form the opposite habit. It does not matter how improbable or how far away this realization may see, or how dark the prospects may be, if we visualize them as best we can, as vividly as possible, hold tenaciously to them and vigorously struggle to attain them, they will gradually become actualized, realized in the life. But a desire, a longing without endeavor, a yearning abandoned or held indifferently will vanish without realization.

Pages:360

Self Help   ISBN: *1-59462-644-8*   *MSRP $25.45*

QTY

The Rosicrucian Cosmo-Conception Mystic Christianity *by Max Heindel* ISBN: *1-59462-188-8* **$38.95**
The Rosicrucian Cosmo-conception is not dogmatic, neither does it appeal to any other authority than the reason of the student. It is: not controversial, but is: sent forth in the, hope that it may help to clear.. New Age/Religion Pages 646

Abandonment To Divine Providence *by Jean-Pierre de Caussade* ISBN: *1-59462-228-0* **$25.95**
"The Rev. Jean Pierre de Caussade was one of the most remarkable spiritual writers of the Society of Jesus in France in the 18th Century. His death took place at Toulouse in 1751. His works have gone through many editions and have been republished... Inspirational/Religion Pages 400

Mental Chemistry *by Charles Haanel* ISBN: *1-59462-192-6* **$23.95**
Mental Chemistry allows the change of material conditions by combining and appropriately utilizing the power of the mind. Much like applied chemistry creates something new and unique out of careful combinations of chemicals the mastery of mental chemistry... New Age Pages 354

The Letters of Robert Browning and Elizabeth Barret Barrett 1845-1846 vol II ISBN: *1-59462-193-4* **$35.95**
by Robert Browning and Elizabeth Barrett Biographies Pages 596

Gleanings In Genesis (volume I) *by Arthur W. Pink* ISBN: *1-59462-130-6* **$27.45**
Appropriately has Genesis been termed "the seed plot of the Bible" for in it we have, in germ form, almost all of the great doctrines which are afterwards fully developed in the books of Scripture which follow... Religion/Inspirational Pages 420

The Master Key *by L. W. de Laurence* ISBN: *1-59462-001-6* **$30.95**
In no branch of human knowledge has there been a more lively increase of the spirit of research during the past few years than in the study of Psychology, Concentration and Mental Discipline. The requests for authentic lessons in Thought Control, Mental Discipline and... New Age/Business Pages 422

The Lesser Key Of Solomon Goetia *by L. W. de Laurence* ISBN: *1-59462-092-X* **$9.95**
This translation of the first book of the "Lernegton" which is now for the first time made accessible to students of Talismanic Magic was done, after careful collation and edition, from numerous Ancient Manuscripts in Hebrew, Latin, and French... New Age/Occult Pages 92

Rubaiyat Of Omar Khayyam *by Edward Fitzgerald* ISBN:*1-59462-332-5* **$13.95**
Edward Fitzgerald, whom the world has already learned, in spite of his own efforts to remain within the shadow of anonymity, to look upon as one of the rarest poets of the century, was born at Bredfield, in Suffolk, on the 31st of March, 1809. He was the third son of John Purcell... Music Pages 172

Ancient Law *by Henry Maine* ISBN: *1-59462-128-4* **$29.95**
The chief object of the following pages is to indicate some of the earliest ideas of mankind, as they are reflected in Ancient Law, and to point out the relation of those ideas to modern thought. Religion/History Pages 452

Far-Away Stories *by William J. Locke* ISBN: *1-59462-129-2* **$19.45**
"Good wine needs no bush, but a collection of mixed vintages does. And this book is just such a collection. Some of the stories I do not want to remain buried for ever in the museum files of dead magazine-numbers an author's not unpardonable vanity..." Fiction Pages 272

Life of David Crockett *by David Crockett* ISBN: *1-59462-250-7* **$27.45**
"Colonel David Crockett was one of the most remarkable men of the times in which he lived. Born in humble life, but gifted with a strong will, an indomitable courage, and unremitting perseverance... Biographies/New Age Pages 424

Lip-Reading *by Edward Nitchie* ISBN: *1-59462-206-X* **$25.95**
Edward B. Nitchie, founder of the New York School for the Hard of Hearing, now the Nitchie School of Lip-Reading, Inc, wrote "LIP-READING Principles and Practice". The development and perfecting of this meritorious work on lip-reading was an undertaking... How-to Pages 400

A Handbook of Suggestive Therapeutics, Applied Hypnotism, Psychic Science ISBN: *1-59462-214-0* **$24.95**
by Henry Munro Health/New Age/Health/Self-help Pages 376

A Doll's House: and Two Other Plays *by Henrik Ibsen* ISBN: *1-59462-112-8* **$19.95**
Henrik Ibsen created this classic when in revolutionary 1848 Rome. Introducing some striking concepts in playwriting for the realist genre, this play has been studied the world over. Fiction/Classics/Plays 308

The Light of Asia *by sir Edwin Arnold* ISBN: *1-59462-204-3* **$13.95**
In this poetic masterpiece, Edwin Arnold describes the life and teachings of Buddha. The man who was to become known as Buddha to the world was born as Prince Gautama of India but he rejected the worldly riches and abandoned the reigns of power when... Religion/History/Biographies Pages 170

The Complete Works of Guy de Maupassant *by Guy de Maupassant* ISBN: *1-59462-157-8* **$16.95**
"For days and days, nights and nights, I had dreamed of that first kiss which was to consecrate our engagement, and I knew not on what spot I should put my lips..." Fiction/Classics Pages 240

The Art of Cross-Examination *by Francis L. Wellman* ISBN: *1-59462-309-0* **$26.95**
Written by a renowned trial lawyer, Wellman imparts his experience and uses case studies to explain how to use psychology to extract desired information through questioning. How-to/Science/Reference Pages 408

Answered or Unanswered? *by Louisa Vaughan* ISBN: *1-59462-248-5* **$10.95**
Miracles of Faith in China Religion Pages 112

The Edinburgh Lectures on Mental Science (1909) *by Thomas* ISBN: *1-59462-008-3* **$11.95**
This book contains the substance of a course of lectures recently given by the writer in the Queen Street Hall, Edinburgh. Its purpose is to indicate the Natural Principles governing the relation between Mental Action and Material Conditions... New Age/Psychology Pages 148

Ayesha *by H. Rider Haggard* ISBN: *1-59462-301-5* **$24.95**
Verily and indeed it is the unexpected that happens! Probably if there was one person upon the earth from whom the Editor of this, and of a certain previous history, did not expect to hear again... Classics Pages 380

Ayala's Angel *by Anthony Trollope* ISBN: *1-59462-352-X* **$29.95**
The two girls were both pretty, but Lucy who was twenty-one who supposed to be simple and comparatively unattractive, whereas Ayala was credited, as her Bombwhat romantic name might show, with poetic charm and a taste for romance. Ayala when her father died was nineteen... Fiction Pages 484

The American Commonwealth *by James Bryce* ISBN: *1-59462-286-8* **$34.45**
An interpretation of American democratic political theory. It examines political mechanics and society from the perspective of Scotsman James Bryce Politics Pages 572

Stories of the Pilgrims *by Margaret P. Pumphrey* ISBN: *1-59462-116-0* **$17.95**
This book explores pilgrims religious oppression in England as well as their escape to Holland and eventual crossing to America on the Mayflower, and their early days in New England... History Pages 268

QTY

The Fasting Cure *by Sinclair Upton*　　　　　　　　　　　　　ISBN: 1-59462-222-1　**$13.95**
*In the Cosmopolitan Magazine for May, 1910, and in the Contemporary Review (London) for April, 1910, I published an article dealing with my experi-
ences in fasting. I have written a great many magazine articles, but never one which attracted so much attention...　New Age/Self Help/Health Pages 164*

Hebrew Astrology *by Sepharial*　　　　　　　　　　　　　　ISBN: 1-59462-308-2　**$13.45**
*In these days of advanced thinking it is a matter of common observation that we have left many of the old landmarks behind and that we are now pressing
forward to greater heights and to a wider horizon than that which represented the mind-content of our progenitors...　Astrology Pages 144*

Thought Vibration or The Law of Attraction in the Thought World　ISBN: 1-59462-127-6　**$12.95**
by William Walker Atkinson　　　　　　　　　　　　　　　　　　　　　*Psychology/Religion Pages 144*

Optimism *by Helen Keller*　　　　　　　　　　　　　　　　　ISBN: 1-59462-108-X　**$15.95**
*Helen Keller was blind, deaf, and mute since 19 months old, yet famously learned how to overcome these handicaps, communicate with the world, and
spread her lectures promoting optimism. An inspiring read for everyone...　Biographies/Inspirational Pages 84*

Sara Crewe *by Frances Burnett*　　　　　　　　　　　　　　ISBN: 1-59462-360-0　**$9.45**
*In the first place, Miss Minchin lived in London. Her home was a large, dull, tall one, in a large, dull square, where all the houses were alike, and all the
sparrows were alike, and where all the door-knockers made the same heavy sound...　Childrens/Classic Pages 88*

The Autobiography of Benjamin Franklin *by Benjamin Franklin*　　ISBN: 1-59462-135-7　**$24.95**
*The Autobiography of Benjamin Franklin has probably been more extensively read than any other American historical work, and no other book of its kind
has had such ups and downs of fortune. Franklin lived for many years in England, where he was agent...　Biographies/History Pages 332*

Name	
Email	
Telephone	
Address	
City, State ZIP	

☐ **Credit Card**　　　　☐ **Check / Money Order**

Credit Card Number	
Expiration Date	
Signature	

Please Mail to:　Book Jungle
PO Box 2226
Champaign, IL 61825
or Fax to:　　　630-214-0564

ORDERING INFORMATION

web*: www.bookjungle.com*
email*: sales@bookjungle.com*
fax*: 630-214-0564*
mail*: Book Jungle PO Box 2226 Champaign, IL 61825*
or PayPal *to sales@bookjungle.com*

Please contact us for bulk discounts

DIRECT-ORDER TERMS

**20% Discount if You Order
Two or More Books**
Free Domestic Shipping!
Accepted: Master Card, Visa,
Discover, American Express

www.ingramcontent.com/pod-product-compliance
Lightning Source LLC
LaVergne TN
LVHW081326060426
835511LV00011B/1885